VAN
GOGHING

All inquirers should be addressed to:

Book Savvy International
1626 Clear View Drive, Beverly Hills California 90210, United States

Hotline: (213) 855-4299
https://booksavvyinternational.com/

Ordering Information:
Amount Deals. Special rebates are accessible on the amount bought by corporations, associations, and others. For points of interest, contact the distributor at the address above.

Printed in the United States of America.

ISBN-13	Paperback	978-1-958876-42-8
	eBook	978-1-958876-43-5

Library of Congress Control Number: 2022919704

VAN GOGHING

RECOVERY TOWARD LOVE

GREGG K. JANN

Book Savvy International
Success is waiting for you...

To My Mother, she was Fun and Wonderful

To My Father and my step mother Nancy, for
dad is The Most Important Man I Knew

To Siblings, Nieces and Nephew, and to Extended
Family I love you and keep you in my prayers,

I'm sorry for In Vivo Non-Communication for GIGO:
for I not hearing talking between us while younger.

Van Goghing Gregg, For He Loves (Women) Always, Now with Brighter Colors in a Royal App.

Gregg Loves, in looking for women—for a wife or partner even in money places like church and politics

Chapter 1

A Young Hero Unrecognized This Way Through

Singing a peace song later published, this immensely turned on my older friend to play music while in I was in third grade introducing him to public school as we walked on our way to school with brothers/ friends. I remember singing it on the corner where the junior high school is on the way to Village elementary. That song made it to fame during Vietnam, perhaps one of the first protest songs. My Dad did not set up a trust for me, even if he knew I sang a song first and originally, like "Peace Corps" as a toddler.

Trusts in financial terms using lawyers may be too much water under the bridge for my past singing in Nebraska, any Einstein enhancement into the social relativity theory while I talked about it in Grade 1 in front of a Chinese substitute teacher, and for Dad who had a Christian leadership career being a Minister later in New York City setting up throughout the nation. Maybe my father was cautious of preemption by his youngest son singing beautiful and saying wonderful words and ideas like a seldom conversant prodigy. I think I was preempted for my early "song larking" by religion, and this abridement is another way for sacrifice I documented previously like religious persecution in social discrimination or church prosecution of the state's law and courts keeping me away from money.

I was unrecognized all my life except for 2 friends while young for the most part. I loved my youth with Dad grounding in cultural impact as minister. I can't remember the name of that song I first sung at the corner of the junior high school walking on the way to Village. Neither do I know who printed up the words and tune in sheet music, who performed the song in some underground cinder block or type of hut or yurt in Northern California, or who forwarded my talent to the person/group who recorded it. "Is that you walking, Ed" was my college Republican friend who I knew for a few years afterward as I sometimes think of editors who kept me printed up too. I "larked" this song (later sung by Michael Jackson) at the Oakland basketball stadium around 2005 as we were leaving the game with his son hoisted high on his shoulders for the last time, I saw him. I still have the poster almost the whole cheerleader squad signed still on my bedroom inside closet door 12 years ago now. I heard this more completed singing first on E Street across my business bank and near the Library while listening to rock radio in my Kia Soul+ sounding like a cold warrior making speeches and surviving corruption from care and theft of my college major.

I was not given input/feedback in lines of communication in writing or orally of my songs and words and ideas taking off like a rocket from me to its mass society impact. I bet sometimes everything I said was taken, in a freaky deal of a large conglomerate prodigy and Protestant Christian icon or just stolen making me sacrifice like Martyr for Sainthood as a demur Protestant Christian. I was denied age of consent and communicative information to my head and heart from every one, and it strikes me as an injustice if I was poisoned as well as denied social supports early on now corrected in original family but not ordinary people. Of course, it is an injustice.

It's not good or funny to be famous while poor, or having poverty of social supports like I think Chico and The Man star was too young. Assistance in gaining emotion strength inside and getting family well to you and relating with close interconnections are also necessary and difficult in my situation so family is protected, cared for, and forgiven by all. Assignment by District Attorney for a young girlfriend relationship sounds counter to prison reform, by a fairness justice complement for good and distinguished people to get enough while the Alcohol. Anon. crowd does its thing to its people. It adds to costs and effort for fairness justice, if we make a push to rehab and reform socially convicts and inmates, that we spend capital and where withal to give care and attention to good people in communication practice.

I have on occasion thought I should sue for respect. First aim was County of Sonoma for labeling me a consumer as I was appointed to serve on the Mental Health Board. I did not know of the criminal justice and substance abuse dominance of the mentally ill departments and psychiatry departments when I started my career involvement in behavioral health and stigma busting.

It feels when I get socially active it did take legal word to include me, or the fighting off of the system. It's not conducive to Paul to sue within church, yet I am a known injustice to mental health parts and some former management employees.

Did I win Len Eshmont Most Motivational Player on JV Montgomery football teams? One year I received a Letter block in my sophomore year, but the next year I did not attend the award ceremony. The class I fell backward in sports was sophomore when I was a junior, and once I graduated the teachers led a strike. They screwed the schools by not paying teachers enough, with the only way to own a home was to join the military and get a loan that way before teaching or marrying someone wealthy who could live in our small city long enough. Not telling me I won an award, even though I expected to, is one factor in a bad school year when senior year arrives.

I liked non-violent rules to football, in that no fighting or intentional injury hitting. Playing hard prevents injury. I was tough and painful on the field, as I rammed my helmet into opposing linemen head on, my force to their helmet. This hurt me and gave concussions to both participants to do this. I would get up quickly to shake off the confusion and pain in my head as I needed to carry the ball often as a fullback. My other trick was in the open field and I classically used straight-arming on linebackers and DBs facemasks as I broke for more yards down the field.

I was only tough in football, and incredibly shy. More than shy is what I repeated as an adult getting care. Back in school I didn't say a word and couldn't banter small talk. Not with-standing my silent friends and always the discriminating school rules, I blame khaki green teeth, as I clammed up not getting comments and teasing about them and became khaki green teeth. I also used my green teeth as a civil rights example without leadership to me. I don't know if others used green teeth in a diversity acceptance program. My father had a sermon on Kermit the Frog for differences I hope to appreciate for kindness, acceptance, and Christianity.

In the 7th Grade I started anti-segregation on drugs as you may know. Maybe this was a bad rap for me, as I talked to hard core pot heads and drinkers to encourage non-violence as I stated previously. I suppose they used it like marketing in parties and encouraged socializing customers and to be like-minded for friendship. I never intended to smoke pot or take any hard drugs, which I didn't. Rough people here kept the nice youth intimidated from being friendly with me, and I was liberal and adult in politically social views but fragile and brittle in coolness interpersonally.

The DA's who worked with my legal secretary employee mom should have treated me to a lady friend. I was later broken and injured even poisoned, and I was not emotionally supported like a girlfriend relationship at any time. It was great original family stepped in at 45 years old or so, after GIGO which is Moral Therapy. I started MT on my own and designed my initiation of it (GIGO wasn't nice). It wasn't family role to get a person a girlfriend, but social kindness and support that does not cloture in carrying out support can be done in extraordinary life circumstances. Was I known to law enforcement and teachers, even statewide officials for heroics I thought were hidden? I was told the Trailside Strangler incident was classified when I researched my past for a book, and I'm not sure the government even has my name associated. I was 15 and a forced technical virgin in no eye sight without having had sexual intercourse yet.

Was the trailside strangler a big, widespread enemy? When we backpacked (my brother and a set of brothers who were friends with me), were the youngsters around Pt Reyes protesting for land rights and against the resident eminent domain laws where Sir Francis Drake landed? A Russian Czar relation lives in a town near there like Bolinas. We just had a killing of a Yogi teacher in the paper in October 2015. Weird civil laws and presumed justice to somebody foreign is at a National Seashore with community codes for a place very close to gayness and the big city population of tough.

To continue for A Jann Plan in the short story in Chapter 5 referred as Museum and Hill Running, or better specifically Pt. Reyes and Dissociating the Hillside Strangler, I did not write too unusual extremes that took re-memory from a great time in A Jann Plan. Here it is, with hopes to not further punishment if I ever was for not testifying or for participating in stopping the criminal acts of a mass murderer.

There was a man waiting for me at my brother's car as I surprised myself for being alone after alleged gruesome incident at the bluff. It was an armed kidnapping by a mass murderer that I blithely carried on with subconscious shell to keep me quiet for 30 years. It's too weird in my mind what I think in unreal mode, as I'm proven to be a non-violent hero with adult politics and talked peace in high school. I flipped out with great speeches as we arrived in my brother's car to set out as I was looking for a platform.

I believe a voice came over the radio we did not have turned on as we drove in past Pt Reyes Station. My brother dropped his head like a black out, and I put my hand on the wheel and his arm to think I was steadying the driver with one hand. He soon came to, as I never deciphered the words on the radio. It was sophisticated.

The two friends acted nervous on the first night as I think back and gauge differently the mood, and like 4th member didn't see me.

When I sat with butt placement carefully near the cliff the 2nd day in the morning, it took a while to realize older friend could have been running away to escape encroachment and evil harm as I read in the newspaper before leaving. He was like that, and his personality eventually alerted me to what I'm thinking. Thank him for that bit of non-violence handling of a tragedy in the making.

After older friend returned from standing and yelling at the cliff, an outline of a person invisible like grey looking clear glass dropped fishing line. He appeared to accidentally step off the cliff. He made no sound, and some hidden sense I knew I was in danger like my friends and brother. I always thought he was real.

I got courage and ran to my brother. He was lying face up in his red boxing shorts and I stabbed small his neck with a knife I took out of my pocket. I was thinking I was choking him with tied fishing line in a trap by the man image going over the cliff. My brother made a face and exclaimed from his sleep and rest.

Then I don't know who broke the neck of 4th Member's alleged gay rapist. It seems our instruction from the voice in the car radio, besides for my brother to keep his keys outside the parked vehicle as the practice, was for 4th Member and all of us to lie face down with his underwear up. Criminal was on friend's back crouching.

My brother is stronger, and I wasn't adult enough to know Geneva Convention rules. I then saw, or think back and now think so, a large knife drop from 4th Member's alleged rapist. The girl, or boy, picked it up as she sat on older friend's back as he was lying face down next to his brother. She sliced a cut on his upper leg close to his testicles from behind. The demise of her also is unknown to me. She was probably stabbed to near death in over powering by someone between my brother and me, leaving older friend bloody which I did not see the blood just knew it was there.

I believe I took off my Oh-What-The-Hell-Shirt, as Cosmopolitan magazine, which was one of my teenage readers, seemed to call my flannel shirts. I tied it around older friend's leg up high and told him to apply pressure to keep from bleeding too much.

Then friends and family left, I don't know if together, with me lying there. I may have told them to hide in these hills and talk to no one. The dead or injured alleged gay rapist and accomplice in attempted murder may have been dumped off the cliff if we were strong and hid evidence from the horse hooves in the Chronicle coverage of Mt. Tam murders. I did ask my oldest brother if it was safe back home a few days ahead of time, before we left for Pt Reyes as Mt Tam has a different feel to me from distance and no association.

I got up and thought 4th Member was with me for a long while on running back to the car.

The person at my brother's driver seat was probably the horseman who ran back counter clockwise on the trail. I don't know if my friends and family saw him, as I did not when I heard a horseman running his horse calling commands as I was on the mountaintop with the back packs soon after the girl in my class and her team of horsemen passed in crossing.

I sat in the car with my back pack in the trunk. I did not say anything about who I was with, as I could have imagined my brother's face in a Capgrass Syndrome overlay and am usually silent the whole time in normal mode way back when.

As I returned to Santa Rosa, the driver used a radio I believe to talk to people, which may be why my 2nd book also thinks it could be a police car like the size of the conspiracy Mariners run. He crammed my head low with is hand, which I originally in writing thought was a screen. When arriving in Santa Rosa in evening or nightfall, we were perhaps in Franklin Field cemetery area or Hoen Avenue or Yulupa as I had ID or maybe not. The kidnapper pointed his gun up. I rushed and shot him in glory or gory memory, as I really don't know what he did. He didn't rape me or do forcible oral copulation.

Is there a picture of a dead man that week in Santa Rosa in my brother's car? I can verify with a coach or his brother I got my brother back, without knowing or ever talking about the incident as the friends survived too. A good reminder for my mind today and used decades later was my older friend showing me his scar on his upper leg one time in our lives, and I did not realize what it meant and we didn't say it then either.

Chapter 2

Participation Did I Say This? Indubitably

I participate, therefore I am.

– Janus and Dubioso in The Empathic Civilization, by Jeremy Rifkin

I read the above quote when working in the church office, after folding the bulletins, between answering calls, and stopping in documenting rents that I collected for the church that are received for AA groups. I was not paid for this church work, but was previously as a teenager while a safe keeper and custodian for the trustees for highest pay claim in high school keeping the job in computer science junior college. This quote started my re- memory process in my mental health recovery, as I thought long, deep and hard on whether I said this philosophy tidbit first for history shifting. It's worth shifting me. Above quote started difficult contemplation for Book II in my efforts to record where I've been and the IP is real, and getting sane and talking with people about my past and in love with the present requires the firming up of assumptions of quote.

Van Goghing Gregg is growing and learning interpersonal interaction, with love next up on the plate. Learning after reading this quote why I was silent, lived in hiding, and grew a virgin exoshell even with medicine induced Asperger's all took a powerful antidote to crack my mental case by myself and with some medicine punishments. I kept on wondering if I said the above quote first and originally, or if I can get rightful credit with a philosophy and political commentary book author career underway. I'm trying that now at the least if not most.

I thought I told my brother under pressure this quote very young in elementary school, even maybe also what is taken to be Descartes credited to the age of reason centuries ago. He said, "I think therefore I am" in what could be like the city council passing the credit around so government says it's good to take turns as a limiter. Maybe thinking now in mourning of my Mother's death that I talked excellently and "robald" whenever a youth even pre-5 saying that I was destined for greatness inherently with this participation blurb from my heart with task with every meaning of a critical thinking royal play act. I had a great background dedicated to the ministry of Christ as more than simply an occupation to start conversation in my family team made by Reverend father and mother. It's the talking of intelligent peer counseling to Nancy my step mother for 25 years in her marriage to my father marked to the day of her death, which words I put together mean healing arts even in out of career context of a caring heart turned more like it is in active expression. I explained much younger that even if I don't make varsity team in basketball, I can still be a basketball player taking his heart in the game seriously. Playing as a youth was at stake, because Vietnam was going on and I believed in children and wanted the creative, joyful spirit of my innocent youth to be strengthened. Most thought we should be adults, and I was in front of news programming and Norman Lear TV to the best of my understanding as a young person.

I was a basketball player with players ad hoc in pick-up games, and the varsity team did not beat my philosophy as we wished not to fight amongst ourselves. All I was were youth sports, and my major thing was football. I also played on the playgrounds and in the parks in summer for lob pitch baseball like Peanuts. Hiking was a loved outlet too, as I said.

It is not just additionally that I was a news carrier paperboy for 18 months bridging junior and senior high school, delivering newspapers with pedal power and collecting subscription fees at customers' door. I serviced my franchise ownership on my own paying the bill wholesale to the big regional paper impressing no one but mother to this day 40 years afterward. Add news carrier in past to college editorials I wrote in newspapers and you find a Business Right to the internet owner manager I tried to be with my business system analyst BS from a good business and computer school.

I was dichotomy thinking to prove myself and said so out loud to close friends I kept loyal to as a youth. Active unofficially, and not active or more sedentary other hours kept the faith of a philosopher even or mostly then. What do you think more about, if you are participating as intellectual, which doesn't sound like you if not reading the New Yorker or going to museums or playing a musical instrument. Learning sexual technique from magazines like Cosmo builds thinking in mental planning about Objective One, with learned ability even virgin style is what is popular.

What does a straight, heterosexual prove about not knowing the girls? I didn't talk to them, and they didn't converse with me. I participated in fantasy making me know that I was for women only, and wish fulfillment in keeping goals to be successful for the day we intermixed. Studying for scholarships, going to college even traveling away to school, and working jobs all meant potential in me and wanting to talk to women when I had something I knew I could say. Being chaste until 39 ½ years old sounds like I participated in priesthood to those I talked with, and I did that too off hand even after later FT raping/forcemeat I didn't know I was experiencing. I was killer in accomplishment and write including religion. I talked a lot about politics and religion trying to set up something new in civil rights for Protestant denominations. I find They not US Religions can't even talk about it, or Church of One Kind uses name calling perhaps poison to maim and control people of ideas and innovative practice.

I participated more with my imagination and thought resolve to keep in contention for more life that I participated in. It's called vision, like a goal, and I did this including for others more than my weekends meant for fun and relaxation. I was on boards and commissions, even elected to advance children while on a school board. My participation encouraged imagination and creativity and morals and interpersonal interaction and careers. This school board era while I was elected and more recent times I say I did movie making with others stealing my ideas unauthorized. No Sainthood to thief, but true credit can help see I am most like one. Saint to origin, knight for new, nude credits recognized precious and monetary both. I wish for needs filled and life greatly to be enjoyed now to counter emasculation and sacrifice, Knighthood for fighting for fun, love, and money I wish with peace to us like I work on.

I have life story that is usually denied to workers in their daily grudge against the talent of society. I say that previous sentence defensively so no one feels sorry for me as I made the most progressive history making since President Kennedy and war and recessions, yet I know it sounds like an asshole except for people like Reagan. Clients in recovery are not liked, not just "no smile" Gregg as I was suffering participating in local politics but most consumers hurt though breaking the law. The only thing in common as when I am or was Chair of the Mental Health Board was an expensive balance sheet not your own so it's controversial when human rights are opposed by aforementioned Asshole to this day by most prominent Republicans as a policy for US and internationally.

It's more than just matters to explain from the heart, in words spoken or written, the feelings from the "me" of my actions. The original source perspective designer and philosopher get to wrack his brains trying to find truth and himself and more even great wealth. I guess it keeps me committed voluntary on free will to get treated, when doctors don't understand almost famous in a client worth most freedom for legal contributor not just mental health like employment rights.

I will find her, hoping for "-us" part to not deny me. Mom warned me late that women took me, when I was a bit of a sour puss in self deprecating reporting to her and with clergymen blindness not understood by medicine. You don't want anyone facetious saying you're nothing, like the only thing the law means in this world is your money to him without explanation. That's politics and unethical practices. "What's in it for me" doesn't block history like we experienced progression if you do hard at it. Greed and lack of care to others like the public do harm what is good that we have already and limit potential to our human stock. Honest crediting getting all the money its worth to original source is important to have to source and carries forth a better country in a reform measure.

Eleanor Rigby from NE a Knight

I don't know if I started or sang enough of the Beatle's song Eleanor Rigby first and originally but strongly recollect this particularly and larking is a bona fide way for groupies having sex to community to studios to each get their lyrics into "vinyl." This song is on their

Revolver Album in 1966, and I was pre-five in my re-memory when I looked it up recently. Songs are the hardest larks to remember, as the excitement of singing and the overbearing overplay of music and listeners make any initial singing recede into the thinking cap. Songs are feelings at this young age, and this pure joy of larking it out often does not have a performance contract to get paid money on this side of the negotiation table as the performer goes about the status quo in running the business end.

I remember a few years ago that I had I visited other churches with my Dad the minister while we were in Nebraska. I entered one particular church in our steeple chasing matches, and joined a group of two of music teacher and singer/student maybe piano. I got the name of the young teenager or some facsimile person and blurted out enough bars of this song for credits stolen. I probably never told my dad and this group official probably or may be a secret to have informed my parents as the song spread.

The thing with silence is I am blocked from family if they ever knew. I don't know if I will ever get the truth from that church about my singing much. Eleanor Rigby brings into my life acknowledging self-fulfilling prophesy in loneliness and no mirror of relationship and fantasy resulting with emptiness. Great American medal was called the same thing by a brother in predicting I would be disabled when about grade 3 for its tribute to ASL and hopefully all great hurt or disabled achievement making lemonade out of lemons.

October 3, 2014
Actress,

San Diego August 10th or so—meet personally or discuss a character for female lead—sisterhood, phantom wife or lover? The women are creative to portray behind the back support, the main man is historic with book soon to be published. I am a self-made Marquis

Who Who in America, and want an explicit agreement to work together using direction from Hollywood on what character you'd like represent in your acting.

Mom always thought I was "special", said I was "cute" often; "stud muffin" by football starring player and overall tough and quality defensive and running back in high school. When I was your age I developed schizo-affective disorder, I think from a poisoning but I'm not sure. Part of the credits search is I want to learn how I got disabled mentally and lived religiously without and suffering for some odd 30 years—emotional supports weren't there much young even though it was a good professional family between a national minister father who moved work to Manhattan and my mother who worked 25 years in the District Attorney's office. There are exciting stories in A Jann Plan of my youth and the outdoors being life threatening to me. Perhaps a mass murderer getting even with me as team work from Marin (I don't know if the sheriff even knows my testimony in A Jann Plan which I just couldn't bear to tell them nothing), or Canada punishing me for molesting a bear family hands on physically as I wrestled after playing with the big one until I was nearly smothered under a picnic table nearly 17 years old.

You're somebody special too. You are a big star making a difference, making people happy with insight into humanity, grounded social skills, and what we need to do to answer our challenges. Your interviews are interesting and provide hope by you being a different person that most Hollywood or even mainly women in the world out there. A natural life with herbs is the nature lifestyle I talked about in my backpacking and camping—even in performance as cooking pancakes unique on a stove in classroom. Taking care of yourself naturally in wilding is an interest I had that we share in common from my past—those frightening experiences I had as a teenager left my wilding undeveloped in the bud with the business degree and not to develop until a healing young woman comes along my way.

You are healing like my daughter. I never had family other than originally who is getting closer to me in my health, befitting a solo act who tried to be monogamous and chaste until Miss Right came into his life because I was conservative morally and she would think I was special. The sex opportunities I did not partake in all my life except a major drubbing in sullying me during a unionization struggle at the group home employment in the Bush II era (a potential movie subject time period in my life, touching church is a question for you) You show in your portrayals and characters chosen a highlight of youth that I can live vicariously safely without damage. I am not damaging to you in feeling, am I?

"Different "actresses playing your part in the movies in Santa Rosa, and different BDs in the teen nudity romp going down at the theater in Blue Ray now make me take a second look at your pretty face. Healing the hole, I had from isolation is your career scripting, and the looks presumed you not a Team heal Capgras Transference or so in that I am more aware. I did not recognize different women in my actual life in 2 work jobs due to my working disability, and a major league in love who I asked to marry was actually different women over a decade. I don't know how many she was, as I only saw her once a month or so. Embarrassing to me now and disqualifying to my family harming my Luther Burbank style wishes for a younger wife in marriage who works on my Saint's right for legacy, on top of wrong ends of the work force unionization recognition. I seem to be better after looking at your nude clips at the Sonoma County Library (Charles Schulz Peanuts in from Santa Rosa too), in distinguishing different people. I don't know if you are the real actress showing nudity and bear naked chests. I subscribe to Playboy and Time magazine for a new magazine. Don't show up in my paper as a whore—and to me for us as a lover and business associate who gives me direction and head is ideal.

I have a health business license, some repute in mental health and a trademark in mental health services—in your big cover in

Time—you can look for a quote to support your meaningfulness in caring through your career verbiage and emotional content of your movies selections and coupling points.

Gregg's Global Warming History

It mattered to me my brother Scott wanted to be an astrophysicists and mastered all the science he could get his hands on through the JC. Looking through his fine telescope, the most beautiful thing I have seen is the first time I saw Saturn and its rings at an unusual night time clear. He usually talked science to me, like he was going to get a fellowship teaching to get through PhD grad school when he was older.

Yes, one of my sisters who was older than me had a phase where she didn't speak on the phone at least when passersby came by in the house. I grabbed the phone at one of these times that she answered, and heard a 'Chinese male voice' ask this end of the line after my "hello", should Scott be an astronaut or man a telescope. I said no, because he was mean. This was when I was about 9. I probably blew all chances, with the Vietnam War going on and him preparing his future draft card induction if such were the case. I don't know if this sore point caused lots of silent treatment to me, all the time from many and from his unfriendly influences.

No talk to me could have been discrimination and persecution for talking up religion in my own way, even if others couldn't mistake my playing philosopher compared to my minister dad. (What about the eye drops story in our side yard at this young age told to me by a beautiful woman coworker in social rehab, reminding me of when I may have introduced social responsibility to care about people like he knew and to care about mission in me like him preaching at the National Monument on my request, or was it this sister or some other reason for Dad the minister to preach at

Sequoia? Adding to Christian belief through concern, and including understanding for others, and offering help to connect where family reasons are to break up any degree of intelligence or lack of caring/ to a lot of it is religion made whole by Donn's youngest son who is Gregg K. Jann. I asked my dad's permission to use his last or my first and last names for a Protestant church just in case, and he felt deeply moved as a professional clergy who made a difference. It doesn't include Royalty (maybe so) but you can reach your ambitions and be anyone in America and be cared for is vital theme I have for previously mentioned in A Jann Plan for Jann Protestantism. Bear Revenant Methodist sounds cheap like a movie, but I think this passed through before way back when to/from my mother as I was beat up in Alberta by a bear family and later got creamed chemically for such extreme punishments like cults of religious persecution, too moral, or too legendary for the other political party. I was someone who stood up in Chemistry class as a student in SRJC and stated I was running for US President like I was one. My current denomination cares about gay ministers, marriage ability for all, and I add now with difficult thinking break through with film and encyclopedia prompts and reminders to help with human crosses against your church member like hurts not just non-depressing songs to sing together. These offerings and my work plans adds two new denominations with standing basis. These two are worth export when professional clergy or lay leaders/elders want to guide to places in Canada, Germany, and even if Russia, and others countries and regions of USA. These may want to be warm regard and US Protestant may want wholeness and practices restoring justice through individuals doing government practices and prevention of harassment. I want Russia to pay me peace dividend like I think I asked as much as a professional football team ($3.5 billion) and rebuilding the South for speaking for the peace side as one voice back when I was called at Chico during the 80s. I deny being like a consumer just asking for favor out of neediness as I never got help, nor jailed, or hospitalized to this day. I teach in non-profit class without yet threatening I may have invented or at least got my contract proposed RFP stolen—the one or 3 I turned into Sonoma County mental health/behavioral health department. Bureaucrats don't work for you, and business may not do it for you any better. It's where the customers are.)

My dad took us, his family of Alice and his children, to Sequoia National Park one year. One Sunday, he preached an ecumenical service in the outdoor "amplitheatre" on simplicity, always impressing me protecting the environment was Christian and that I could do so. A class at Chico State University business school on Environment of the Business System led my term paper on Health benefit costs to society needing to be covered. My school board era definitely created opportunity I took so well to include safety of children with competition rules on emotional well being. The environmental aspect is more easily seen as straight ahead Christian in a more inclusive destiny I carried in my thought pattern.

My brother Scott, this time I know it was at our first Santa Rosa house, had a chemistry of meteorology textbook out. I opened it and saw a diagram on gasses in Earth's atmosphere. I saw a graph with many pollutants and that carbon gasses had an ability to warm our planet, and it was disastrous that it could speed up an ice age like the Polar Ice Caps. I was alarmed and took this book out and told my big brother Scott.

I was probably the first inspiration point to take this hidden knowledge on my intuition out of the chemistry or meteorology textbook and make it publicly known. Soon we had catalytic converters in California. Like most of my source perspective designer originals, I was too young to know for sure how this Global Warming panic hit the streets making cooler cars and changing American gas guzzling to cleaner, alternative energy use. I was always concerned about pollution, not just trash on the creeks, and I was an early advocate to not tool down 4th Street Saturday nights cruising burning fossil fuels putting a hole in the ozone layer. I couldn't explain the ozone part of the problem when I was 10 years old.

I was not cool socially, except I held my ground in directions our county needed to look and even go to make a sustainable future with people getting along better. In emergencies we as one world need to cooperate, prevent disaster, and minimize conflict.

Social Responsibility: Essay by Gregg Jann (AS 1982), Jann Demystifying Affects™ or Jannda.com

Standing up in my Chemistry 1A class at Santa Rosa Junior College, I reported a 60 minutes program and in hind sight a national magazine on Love Canal. Completely appropriate for engineering, science, and doctors students to understand it was wrong of some country like ours to dump chemicals without care into the ground, causing birth defects in high numbers in that community and wherever else this is the practice of chemical dumping of most types.

I started a Social Responsibility plank as an Idea Man for President running for office as soon as possible and with applying my mind for greater business tycoon over environment to include social responsibility. Marriage and family were wanted by me, later or sooner for my conservative morals, and most Christian viewpoints lead this take on social responsibility. I kept up with SR with a damaged health status while attending SRJC in 1981, and soon before graduating with an AS I wrote in the school newspaper starting with an anti-draft essay while feeling down over Presidents Weekend in 1982. One, I was injured and felt mental care could be led by peace attempts and ideology practices, and 2) my computer business major could use a reaching across peace philosophy in connecting computers from building to the next country across the ocean. I proved my peace philosophy in continued newspaper writing at 2 state universities in graduating, and in public newspapers all my adult life. I now write a constructive mental health education blog and have published 2 books, mainly compilations of previously viewed material with new advances in IP for my take on recovery.

Damage caused by uncaring of those scientists and business leaders of Love Canal and similar who should know better was my back end of my big heart for adult policies, and I never expected to work counseling for pay where medicine drugs are used as I did after Chair of the Sonoma County Mental Health Board. I asked for a Social Responsibility class in the instruction in every science class I was enrolled while taking Chemistry 1A for civil engineering or industrial engineering, or well repeated comments by the instructors. I received this principle in being taught, and is what I got thankfully. My business essays and advocacy Jannda.com and medicine in social rehab counseling is and was above board. I did not do the cleaning bed pans of a CO warrior near combat in draft age as my educator Left essay established a futility of drafting soldiers making war bigger and as often without a treaty if drafts of soldier remain.

On Veterans Day that year and not knowing it was an instructional day off, in my Physics 1A class a group of instructors showed a gayness film to our instructors to be courageous for our students to be more understanding which I thought was an OK idea as I sat in attendance. In our city being close to a homosexual center of San Francisco, an instructor I took for computer programming wore women clothing the year after I graduated attending Chico State. This was more serious than a computer lab in the 90s showing a screen of a gay dating web site seeming to be an assignment. While a sophomore, Economics quoted Milton Friedman, a Nobel winner some years previously to 1982, stating business social responsibility was producing what the economy needed without regard to kindness, understanding, or better human rights. I was a grad student at Sonoma State with just a 2nd- BA in Econ, when the school accepted my MBA application but never offered this graduated degree except in marketing materials for recruitment.

Care is what social responsibility boils down to, and is what people need to be human. It requires ethics to do it right. Being denied marriage rights and relationship discrimination due to religious preference, health status, and income problems did not stop my social responsibility accomplishing kindness leadership in policy and code while making history marks at work, on boards, and for election, also as sole proprietor winning a coaching award for marketing ideas even prospective US foreign policy to anti-bullying needs in chemical medicine treatments.

Contact Gregg Jann for award he wants and deserves for caring with ethics. For 2nd book A Jann Plan released World AIDS Day 2014 Non-fiction designs of sources and perspectives in IP advances Election service in non-violence at Piner-Olivet USD And mental health work rights and mental health contributions

Chapter 3

Advocating and Blogging

Cures for Constipation and Act-hole

Submitted by Gregg Jann on Wed, 2014-05-14 10:42

With divinity and toughness, I'm solving problems like an Oakland Raiders quarterback. Burst appendix hoisting an alcoholic brew while horseback back country Utah may impress Al for a high draft pick. There are other ways to stardom, mediocre stats, and too moral except for 2nds.

Jannda.com health business license: Sip hot water or tea for constipation. Set up an appointment with a physician if serious or lasting pain. Leave out long story why you hurt back there, lest charges from delusional to hypochondria to perversion from medical staff.

A doctor's poke in an instant exam upon a question asking help in peer counseling work and for a moribund feeling about discriminated class in stature, made my ass hurt and not walk able days at a time for years. Most any malpractice brainstorm in the course of business in personal life is evil regarding an ungrateful clientele; or overall processing wellness is better for me. 2nd chances need to be taken for a dire need for exercise in requiring a follow up visit.

Prevention and Health

Anti-Psychotic Metabolic Syndrome pre-2003

Thu, 2014-05-29 15:28

Mental Health Meds make consumers gain weight, which some professionals have been reluctant to agree with the findings. Evidence supporting anti-psychotic metabolic syndrome shows a case strong enough for caring doctors to switch meds for at-risk consumers of health conditions of severe obese patients with heart risks and glucose blood sugar threats.

Meds as old as Depakote from 1992 to the early anti-typical anti-psychotics of the early 2000s cause this metabolic syndrome of weight gain.

The suggested replacement med for one discourages appetite in advertisement by doctor. These strange type epilepsy/borderline meds with unproved mood stabilizer effects is prescribed FOR depression when consumer only has manic parts does cause concern. Update: I think this med was prescribed in malpractice for wanting a young girlfriend, who is to say I'm not following in my father's footsteps?

Prevention and Health

Messy Leads to Mental Illness

Thu, 2014-06-19 16:32

Lacking hygiene on the person's body, wearing too worn or dirty clothes, or keeping his room untidy are signs of having schizophrenia if these conditions are worsening. What if the parents, family or peers single out this person for dislike on these charges of unkempt habits during heightened awareness of cleanliness habits? People may rate this person as weird socially, and make him withdraw into anxiety and loneliness until the crowd and family make him take on mental illness full blown. Mental disability can start from simple style and personality differences, or too sweaty playing sports in street clothes.

Later psychiatry steps into gear and administers medication for him to exacerbate his beginnings of his journey into a chemical imbalance. Shouldn't we talk to these people to coach them with gentle love to strengthen our nation and society, instead of abandoning them with exaggerating our reports to doctors or medical association for our own shortcomings in caring for our fellow mankind?

Motivation

Interplay of Christianity and Mental Health

Mon, 2014-07-07 17:18

"Clanging Bells" who change the world they live in are not appreciated as people in US/Christianity law like employment discrimination. Consumers under care by psychiatrists who are leaders of survivors may also be hurt if no family even if loving in making steps in big world changes. Corinthians I:13 seems to need an explanation to community spirited work for goodness and love to you which is what I include with leadership not always pleasant, when individual interpretations may only mean relationship in family to them.

Love your neighbor. The most important commandment for each of all of us in this world of all religions of the world for peace and understanding one another, after those who are Christians of us that must believe in God the father as non law.

Do unto others as you'd have them do unto yourself. Secular elementary school uses this passage to teach politeness and respect for each other. Love and care to disabled difficulty is so much more than shallow appropriate feelings and needs are deeper. The Golden Rule is before and after my religion came along.

Something like bear caring witness is the Bible, which to me means any type of love - individual or whole in heart outlook.

Holistic Community and Perma culture

Phantom Love Proves Illusion in Hard Shell

Tue, 2014-07-29 13:29

Sugar Ray sings Someday, and it is a pretty song that I took to mean my phantom lover relationship who did not converse or talk out loud to me and it goes like this:

Someday when my life has passed me by I'll lay around and wonder why you were always there for me.

She was many women who replaced one another to fool staff, and I did not recognize who she was in particular except I loved someone in her. Eventually we separated while never together in absence after tragic consequences in a peace offering during a workforce fight as I was alone making history as part of union negotiations. I increased worker rights for mental health consumers in my labor economic authorship in group home counseling, voted in by line staff.

I do know I carry love in my heart for far away people from HER. This type of love does carry liability in not recognizing multiple faces in my inexperience thru rough-ass hazing from LA hardcore to mental health system asshole and Catholic priest abuse scandals in the newspaper.

Family and Friends

Town Namesake a Surprise Appreciation

Thu, 2014-08-21 15:31

It's worth another Saudi King (or PRS of a protestant religion) with Beit Jann in Israel named after a famous House of God. It's No Relation to a Druze Icon century ago, but this is fun now. My father was a national minister and did Christian philanthropy for 30 years in Manhattan and through the country for Church Development. I survived a runaway subway attack captured on film as a fun-loving survivor with no teeth. I had them made whiter from a khaki tetracycline stain when a baby. I spoke on needs and not listening to father to unknown Russians at Chico and a posing Libyan terrorist on board hooked up and wired.

I apologize for my silence in my style to not verbally tell people legends that belong to me.

I'm documenting them with nonfiction accounts published October 2014. Recovery was hard on me. Wipe out and suppression made me innocent of any associated harm of my hero whose wasn't all there in presence of mind past.

Advocacy

Feminism, Gender Equality, and Chastity

Wed, 2014-09-24 17:25

The UN HeforShe program for recruiting men to talk with the women in their lives in support of Gender Equality throughout the world is a needed advocacy inclusion. The sexual revolution in the USA was about women's rights in sex, then work; with little adding in caring ability for both genders.

A Kinder, Gentler nation and world includes fresh, inexperienced people and the older generations to express attitude and viewpoint on topics called together. Using poetic license words "sugar and spice", warm regard in developing persons and existentially is lost quality, particularly in War.

The British actress who is the UN Women Goodwill Ambassador needs to remember what I say (FB, NOW political endorsement, life, etc): Does feminism include individuals not in relationship and men who aren't well?

Civil service does not, discrimination in employment harms these, and the social mores say for women to be neither home nor assistance to colleagues if inhumanly chaste or sick.

Homeland into Foreign Policy

A Love Story at the Theater

Tue, 2014-10-14 14:54

The entertainment license of plays, movies, even television permits an enterprising person to build value from the performance. Any creative, critical thinking applied is constructive and belongs to the viewing owner. The audience has an ability to stay true in discussions afterward, or go off on "tangents" with our own meaning and interpretations. Not with health licenses even internet.

Prelude to a Kiss is love in changed person. This play is a little weird, and uncomfortable at SRT on males kissing is punishing. The male lead was a trouper in staying with someone he loved however different his bride was on the honeymoon. Small visual about age spread coupling - take heartfelt notes for Gregg!!

Different people portraying a name games at work new in memory and it was 5 years ago when this was first posted, or movie stars using stand-ins and body doubles on the big screen and in star media make replacement acting usual. Hopefully never de rigueur, switching images affects Santa Rosa with actress Shailene too.

Reviews and Entertainment

Intrapersonal "Shell Leadership"

Thu, 2014-10-30 16:55

Usually communication is seen as a leadership quality, and we also accept success about people more when they use "sweat equity" like work. Learning likability or breaking barriers in communication difficulties, even if their own make up, can be persuasion sell as one form of sweat equity for a worker or leading man.

First in concepts like a scientist and things there, or holding his own history of accomplishments and processing successes of the place can be from introspection. Operating with sensitivity or self reliance like a kind, respected cannonball can lead changes in workplaces.

Contemplating on his experience can be power in that quiet office, from building relating and understanding to creativity mind set. Reflection of his long standing ability can add his lustrous qualifications, and traditional leaders do not know what the Shell leader is thinking as he builds the future.

Critical Thinking Fighting Suppression

Good Reads.com book review by This Owner

Wed, 2015-11-04 14:36

On Goodreads.com, other reviews on Amazon.com, Amazon.in and Google (see inside) Author was too legendary for his silence in hazy forgetting, his hidden actions all add up to like a Saint(or Priest abuse), would cults of religion or governments foreign and domestic poison him like Royalty plumage to steal valuable monetary intellectual property making false origin of famously used works and words?

A Jann Plan makes him competent in Publishing Editor approval in non-fiction of his posting counseling essays over several years, leading into market claims of US America's important business advances by author.

Teach Peace and Creative Accountability is a suggested law, getting ready for ballot for his still existing elected school board work opposite the era's violence on campuses across the nation. Suggestion also counters the "No Credit" of the Reagan era like LA Hollywood does its thing in raiding innocently creative up in Northern California.

Author Gregg K. Jann writes with a health business license in critical thinking for mental health, and is a leader of business rights for consumers of social security, welfare codes, and disabled needs, as well as character education in schools for young people. These combine in the middle subtitle of Creative Origins Advocacy.

Mr. Jann is in Marquis Who's Who in America and lived off most records of pulverizing medicine as an innocent man never hospitalized and is a legal and mental health contributor at the least, if also in a role he was educated to do and as entrepreneur inventing the internet.

Mr. Jann's review on Goodreads
Holistic Community and Perma culture

Addiction Psychology Wrong on Innocent

Thu, 2015-10-29 14:42

Most mental health consumers and providers carry addiction psychology in their practices MO. "It's your fault for choosing immoral options to try to fill your need and now you are stuck repeating them all the time or too much" is on their minds. Anything an addict does in manipulation or motivation has a basis of choosing substances that require behavior to meet false needs, and that behavior is unethical and at its very heart dishonest.

It is wrong to believe from providers, peers, society, or taken inward to blame yourself for a psychotic nervous breakdown that was not caused by substances or illicit behavior. Innocently obtained disability happens, and extremely distinctive in contributing to the field of mental health care through work rights, appointed and elected office, and human justice in ideology practice beliefs.

Don't treat with guilt an innocent man, and don't take my example in treatment and be non-judgmental those who are under addiction psychology.

Prevention and Health

Continues A Jann Plan on AIDS Naming

Sun, 2015-10-04 23:50

Thanks to Avid Reader Davis staff and participants for asking me on my story for naming AIDS. National Alliance for Mental Illness (Sonoma County) acknowledged credit in their weekly news bulletin Friday for A Jann Plan for an educational presentation each month I do for them.

Lying low in hiding from 2 mass killer instances after saying AIDS first and originally (see A Jann Plan, a non-fiction book), I don't know if I was Reagan blacklisted perhaps for Democrat speech maker and for too legendary at 20 years old.

The mass killer incident at the seashore is classified as told to me by a Ranger directly. Both incidents clammed me up and lonely through college, except great "larking' under pressure.

On AIDS looking for a name and not exactly in a newspaper article: "acquired" because I asserted unbelief at mutants, "gay cancer" or "gay pneumonia" needed a name and I related to an indeterminate period not knowing what I suffered from not AIDS in myself nor gay, deficiency in white blood cells an effect, and a syndrome for widespread condition.

Prevention and Health

Curtailment of Rights/Preemption - Abridgement

Wed, 2016-03-09 13:32

Abridgement is curtailment of rights, like less business rights. I have no curtailment of rights, probably due to being one President Reagan speaker first and originally, and some other good things from me. Or am I FOR NOW? I am leading business and labor rights for people on supports like social security against mental health departments with discrimination in their industry. This is picking up where US Presidents who want to be Father left for me to do, where professionals are not humanitarian. In other words, we the People mean more, in ways we do it, not some asshole in government who never built people or organized communities all.

For equal time, I don't approve the Administration's preemption of the Academy Awards with his family and VP statements. I don't know the movie industry, but their business is their business for our meaningful enjoyment - not for someone who wants attention without caring like the usual candidates or like a nude actress.

Property Rights and Ethics

Writing Style for Community Activism

Thu, 2016-10-27 15:27

Language chose rate fmr. faulty syntax by Gregg's creating fresh words never used before in context like AIDS for the famous disease back in 1982 to a slang for sex object now used for SEX IN THE South from when I was a too decent youth.

My philosophy body gets you to think for reader to use mirror of relationship for action. Untrained having better morals, crediting sources for history story BUILDS to truth what was stolen from Gregg. Each sentence in Gregg's blog entries and his books are meaningful alone if not following standard conventions together.

Psychology is a complement, and the sex and coarseness and danger in the sex word choices I designed start or end and are not lost in wonder so they are not philosophy. Morals and truth are.

The vulgar, slang word for sex I invented is "poontang." I stated it on brother's question to deflect immorality. I remember inventing this word in our upstairs loft of a nice house overlooking a private grassy yard with our pool yard at the back end. It was out of the blue, just a word I added to after creating it and that I would regularly speak instead of "pussy," particularly out on the expansive football field at Montgomery while we were in junior high. I don't know how my childhood got to be published in popular fiction and within word encyclopedias saying these fiction sources were predating the raping of my youth as usual exploitation of the media, film and books, and society.

I was late to consider the subway runaway instigated by me as the King of the Head Bobbers as I looked toward shoreline on the Jersey coast near the George Washington bridge, and in basement of 475 upon return I may have started Interlink Self Help Center although it is very unsure I said it except both Dad and myself have been like that. His church development job may have exploited me without words to me, and at first blush I was protected and cared for to make my way out of Dodge City and exploitation upon exploitation as past practice of New Yorkers.

Motivation

Doing Better in Advocacy and Innovation

Fri, 2016-09-09 15:46

For patient/consumers, half the battle for interpersonal relations with relatives is keeping them close to you beginning with some point in time and keeping them from feeling sorry for you. Not complaining is an American strong suit, but with stigma on mental illness perhaps the relatives can be a focus group of test marketing of how to get people to understand you. By talking to family and trying new things for them to be proud of, you can keep a pattern of normalcy denied to immorality, manipulators, and users of the general public.

Trying to add to care with new psychological contributions or coming up with words used copied in arts, technology, and liberal arts like theater, Jannda.com readers can see extraordinary production used commercially in medicine.

Educating on implementing the consumer self help movement is important to carry with you, even if the choir you were preaching to was your extended family both direct and indirect and less so non-profits.

Family and Friends
Prevention and Health

Credit, Managed Care worth Talking

Fri, 2016-09-02 15:20

I came across reading about a man who is both MD and MBA, who wrote a series of articles on giving credit for organizations attributed in the same year of processing my final copyrights for A Jann Plan in 2014. He writes organizational theory and practices for Harvard Business Review and works for a health provider. He could be fair like me, but one trick in management is not to give credit to people managers don't like. Mental Health consumer employees may be difficult in expressing emotions, or disliked morals, or expensive on the ledger sheet, or just short lived staying employed.

I did not know the above author or hear or read of him like he could have Gregg Jann, and the dates may be doctored up to say HBR does not plagiarize from a state universities' educated peer and entrepreneur. Whether starting too low as a patient rights advocate once in the mental health field, or getting forced bad or funny reactions while walking the streets with a purpose whether exercise or a form of work, people who don't believe in property rights often don't credit -particularly progressive history sweeps like union struggles for work rights.

We in the mental health movement need credit given and rewarded for all the parts used in economy and art like diseases I claim.

Property Rights and Ethics

Management Training for Peace Treaty

Sun, 2016-08-21 17:13

For armed services adding, more understanding soldiers can mentor MH consumers to bear responsibility and citizen participation as much as an elected Democrat non-partisan activist. It is like the US Coast Guard to change work to guiding and rehabbing persons with psychiatric disability. Having a Peace Department for pay is a good idea for private and public entities from Washington DC, a second is not maiming for opinion. I extrapolate from a theme on a ship I saw while exploring the mighty Columbia River this past week going to a museum or two.

Taking in necessary US history worth management training programs for bolstering attitude US vs. Them, Near Me, which I knew somewhat in my colleges MIS and in San Francisco. My Sabbath vision planning was also interesting. Commercial enhancement of trade shipping assistance can encourage a Pacific Treaty by Jannda.com to not harm or maim MH consumers who are different as rated by doctors, family, and communities.

Advocacy

It Looks Like the "Gawky", GOCY Revolution

Thu, 2016-07-28 17:58

The Digital Revolution with cell phones, internet and computer of the Information Age does a lot of changes to us. Some of us who are technophobes are less touched by technology, and know our junk mail and payroll have come from computers since at least the 1970s. In my very good business school of Chico State, where we could only be Republicans or fleshy drinkers, not EBU achievers like I was & treated to isolation as a politico. I was told not to use the word "revolution." "Rejoiner" after entry made: I tried to explain my innocence by saying Gloria Steinham's quote and MS Magazine reading could transfer to changes for healing men and women who needed recovery in mental health or any disease. I wasn't a big participant in dorm social life in partying as I hid a lot in my room knowing I was ill with something and did invent a deadly communicable disease name just getting accepted into California state university. I was captain of 2 flag football teams with "Seek Victory" writing by myself on the football we used, including our dorm's women's flag football team. It worked on the dance floor when of age at 22 and continued into Santa Rosa after college before boring nice Sonoma State, for my friends' band and also popular disco era when good rock was playing.

Blog continued: With Hilary Clinton accepting the Democratic nomination tonight, I feel blessed by participating in progressive movements of history although I'm not rich by material wealth. Advocating less pollution and wanting mass transit for elders, 70s and 80s YO to travel; truth to origin in economic larking for songs, movies, and general capitalism endeavors; consumers of all types with more rights with emotional bolstering, and with heart of each for GOCY movement.

Just a good one added here: Gay rights is my victory too, through Reconciling Methodist no signature by me for proven danger issues for being nice and the tit for tat harm in America. Now we all need my school board era and the goal I previously published twice. (No college English, but I am not that bad to include this elected body work thrice here. Read A Jann Plan for Teach Peace school constitution amendment offered for me to include what I need like small business rights for disabled to own and prosper and feel love enough for marriage, or if ever again published Bettering the World for things I want to win for being the only peace voice. I helped to elect a women congressman with no money from me who I asked to be the one "no vote" in a War if ever necessary at the Santa Rosa Democratic Club. Success idears connection based on now I am elected with a killer accomplishment basis in college after my Left editorial was published writing while I was sick and family moving across town same Presidents Day long weekend, as she's her own woman.

Holistic Community and Perma culture

US Vice President or Cabinet Secretary

Wed, 2016-06-29 14:06

A US Constitutional Amendment on Teach Peace and Creative Accountability needs a public dialog on building our young people to develop our nation. Recess in school is free play. Giving educators the ability to design soft skills interaction & exercises for the young to learn both competitive models and supportive non-violent honor social skills is the next step.

TP/CA chaptered in A Jann Plan (other plans are false origin) educates knowing what "you" talk about, understanding emotional well-being interpersonally first from intra- personally, and makes for carrying a more respectful understanding toward each other against bullying. Spreading Teach Peace over time to each of all of our California/American people and making a curriculum Segway teaching us the journeys of our USA progress forwards and some truth to consequences fighting the "good" fights.

Industries will be more honest for its starts, as will legislation know who's larking the idea not just sponsors in the Houses of Government for truer honor. It defeats the purpose of this character Ed for little people amendment to leave out the Creative Accountability portion worth money like education is supposed to work.

Homeland into Foreign Policy

Examples of On Going Dream Realization

Tue, 2016-06-14 13:23

In below entry and previously at times in my licensed company's health services blog, I communicate stability with some good mood suggestions. On-going dream realization or just following up on visualizations help a person's security for activity on a goal felt warmly. ODR holds stronger feelings for wellness.

Keeping those long term goals that entail processing of an entire life situation makes one feel like his illness has not got the better of him. Graduating from college after psychiatric disability starts in earnest, getting jobs with management in the title even sales account executive and assistant manager much, or mature about ending youth at (F. Scott Fitzgerald's) 30 years old by going to church like you wanted to; are all part of Gregg Jann's Ongoing Dream Realization. I utilized community leadership in my life plan in first advocating ODR on a web site for CA's Prop 63 before it was christened the MHSA.

Now I'm real and want ODR relationships of fine lady friends.

Motivation

Singing in Church Keeps from Depression

Sat, 2016-06-11 17:58

Music Therapy works for many types of people, from people with Autism Spectrum Disorders to Mental Illness and tons of others. A professional includes consumers in song selection and helps their client create music. Many areas of functioning are addressed in other areas of his life, for example social, cognitive, physical, etc.

My only anecdotal research experience is within a community of Methodists worship singing in praise of the Lord. It seems like we often sing of Peer Counseling in relating to Jesus, and the songs add to my care. My congregation doesn't talk to me about sins, and I socialize just a little in fellowship and some fundraisers wanting more fun personally.

A consistent source of rotating playlist, some songs I never heard of, keep me stable and safe from feeling depression. This wholesome good spirit guides through reading lyrics on a big screen with the crowd of membership. I am less moved emotionally in security by the churchly joys and concerns of community or the sermons I can hear and remember from the Minister's notes which I appreciate.

Prevention and Health

"Grass Roots Gregg" Part II: Russia?

Tue, 2016-05-03 13:32

Jannda.com blog documented as read in 33 countries past month. Similar to crediting writing with divine inspiration, does Vapor Ware record visits throughout the world without the words read from a mental health angle? Which both positions say one end to another connected is not human forms. Don't deny my body of written work and politico production which is like Adonis to my waitress.

This Guy who is author may have spoken to Soviet Union as the real President during Reagan's term for me to say something young more mature for it to retire and get smaller as a country thereby making a bigger people to them many peaceful ways. I don't know this for sure due to immense pressure on my brain point while I was a silent legend.

Do you have problems with the Far Right taking from students and too youth without their informed permission? A propelling catapult of a human source of speeches, internet, and religious collaring unofficially a lot as a small person trying to make it under unfair conditions may be able drive peace in Europe as I may have appeared to—like did my writings documented in Bettering the World by Gregg K. Jann (out of print) help reduce the size and severity of wars we get into by opposing or banning the military drafts of many nations? Let's get a treaty for my money to me and less so to assistants like even a retired working ambassador could read this. (I liked her pin when I visited San Francisco Legion of Honor where I kissed a girl using hand signals. My pickup line is reported I caught a mass killer following a pattern nearby behind that high hill across the bay and was blinded in this exact experience in front of her and the museum curator at the gift store clerk station. I feel I got a salute of beautiful women wearing more purple of the type of clothing she wore with a woman at each bus stop until the Golden Gate Bridge as I returned to Santa Rosa, CA a few days later.

Homeland into Foreign Policy

(Grass Roots Gregg) Part I: Internet Stolen

Tue, 2016-04-26 14:34

A Jann Plan's cover portrays funny into author's character we took advantage of, and the part with the diagram of the AIDS anti-body included in book for Jann's original naming. Cover face could be journalism sleeping with Jann's market advances never getting past the cutting floor safely in his possession. Using a health business license, author Gregg Jann writes counseling essays and in mental health de-stigma and for property holdings like Social Responsibility and for himself. His business customer service experience shows we can hold to the unknown, unaffiliated first and original source people of enterprises "out there" and well as care for the vulnerable wannabe.

Church and royalty stories add a luster from when this author is ever credited, like internet inventiveness contributor. Told to me that as a country we do not advocate in bible study, and teaching about Peace with soft skills from schools is also within Gregg Jann's Americanism for experience at work and while elected for school board. ("Grass Roots Gregg") worked on the internet during the 80s before the Web was widely used, and was too stolen from, even all the CA legislation.

Property Rights and Ethics
Gregg Jann's blog

Doctor's Punishments for Not Liking

Tue, 2016-02-16 14:06

Whether for trying research on innocents, for ideologically opposed to expensive benefits like Medi-Cal, or for things too hard assed in patient not needing "normal" things for not a usual routine life all are hurt in medical consequences by corrupt prescription in due honest health license. Ever heard "don't worry about it" for inconvenience and discredit of normalcy, and hear the doctor explain reasons, for example patient is not working. Making medicine victims for no significant relationships can't be covered by a boss, but perhaps family can fill discrimination for not a spouse.

Nurses, doctors, psychiatry medical staff all harm mental health clients for a communist life right in the medicine provided to them. Is Bernie out to save MH consumers, do Candidates want to steal A Jann Plan in the banking reforms with non-payment of income, or do we all protest for best care not harm to all?

Prevention and Health

I am Revenant for 1900s Bear Fighting

Fri, 2016-02-05 14:06

In A Jann Plan tucked into the first chapter, I write an account of my bear wrestling in summer 1979 in Banff, BC; which may be in Alberta outside Calgary. It hurt me to the point of near death and I was in trauma. I don't know if I was in Alberta, and I never got the directions nor followed the map straight.

I only saw a cub walking to me as I played with the big bear's face. The full account is in the book already published, with my addition here that I pulled something in the bear's groin and she urinated on my face as she was backward stuffing me into a den type structure. I tell you this for survival as a point I missed in first writing. Maybe bears like light attitude and laughing softly a little too, but I don't know. Don't do it intentionally.

On the drive to Canada, I talked Conscientious Objector with nothing war going on and my family objected. My 20th Century Bear fighting championship continued winning history- making and producing genesis points used mainly in mental health. I determine other fields can be corrected and property and money returned to me in greater amounts for unauthorized use and theft. I was called "Most Revered" by an anxiety case person I respected and she seemed older in her man she made it into Sonoma County Democratic Politics in a local level. I liked her and don't know if she is connected to the movie made of a great 19th Century bear fighter. I told family I wanted a movie made of each Century's champion bear fighter long ago.

I believe I stated in the car going to the capital of Victoria, BC that I said the name of this branch of honor and environment that is Methodism of, "I am Revenant." I was working at CCUM. Bear Revenant is worth Canadian religion of wrestling God or Ogre and is but one reason I think I could have been poisoned to have Schizo-Affective Disorder. Where I was an elected community activist I spread some of my then current ideas with proof somewhere I was stolen. My family doesn't think I fought the bear family, and only acted like I slept with him as they/we abandoned me for the experience as I lay dying hours. I want us all to have Protestant Christian understanding of Methodist, with me a Protestant Religious Symbol making up the true meaning and finally being successful and as healthy as possible.

Homeland into Foreign Policy

Adding Care Wins It - for Big Time Too

Mon, 2016-02-01 14:30

Adding care and a softer heart for people, especially those in your life, is a winner. Spending time with the elderly, as in relations or even volunteering in senior homes, develops patience as a quality inside shown outside. Learning to notice people, like them looking in your eyes for the first time ever, is a game changer.

From getting a recalcitrant complainer to smile and teaching her to talk pleasant on the way to church as you drive her, to wearing a neon rain coat drawing looks on the street, to self revelations on greeting cards that she is nicer to you and in and of itself is making a difference in receiver's inside or the sender if saved for later reading.

Adding care to your lexicon wins awards in business, like Jann Demystifying Affects won 2015 Best of Santa Rosa Award - Training Consultants Category. Years ago Trump Towers won the same award, as did Entrepreneur magazine both in New York different categories. Big Time Takes Care.

Motivation

Personal Acknowledgements:

It was hard to break a forced technical virgin Exoshell. I didn't look down from beautiful women having unknown sex to me in a union fight then to a lab coat for Nobel urology reporting and just think so without seeing normally anything or feeling it at the moment in a burning of no sensation some few times. I have been basically no other challenge been too moral for 40 years of women, so I hope to convince crowd and doctors care to not punish me for a young wife

I someday will be worth when we are more honest about crediting in American economy not always worth money.

The people around in Santa Rosa were bad from jail offenses or gayness, which just isn't me at all. Politics just mostly meant money, and church didn't think I was real enough to socialize. I owe my warmer disposition to my father for talking to me and inviting me to a Giants game for the World Series at his home in Scottsdale/Fountain Hills, AZ—I must have missed 3 playoffs in years before finally seeing 2010 and beyond more recent. Mother mainly.

His last wish was for me to take care of my mother, when earlier was to read the Bible which I do in study, and for me also do the same good things I did before in the 1990s culminating in being an elected school board member. Mom gets less or no verbal punches from my abrasion out of my no regard symbiosis in California and now smiles at me for the first time although talks little due to her infirmary of well past 85. I get a great kick out of being with her. My politics and policy was always kindness and leading with innovation. In person nice and loving I want a complement worth a wife, and I set this aside to live outside my contemplation and stress fracture of a block to do so. Keep reading as my battle was always to get "taller" in success as I read in a teenage reader, but mostly the New Yorkers who are into magazine-making meant money which was denied to me in ignorance past of where I was leading this nation as an unknown small person like a diagnosed Nice Aspie, which is not what clinical medicine diagnosed for me.

Mother passed away at a good age during this my writing processing, and my love to my mother remains good as I expressed gratitude to her for her efforts to make me warmer in the end. She said she would have liked to talk to church and all her friends about me, her son, Gregg Jann being elected to a school board. I was advised to not talk about this and told mother so to protect my themes and plans from recall election before we in California had one in Governor. We need my school board goal for the country to get going and get along with understanding and kindness, not just gay rights but all marriage rates are low and I always had a girl in the back of my mind who I just couldn't reach.

Jannda.com blog entries: For it proves competency in a fight to post strategy with counseling essays

Jann Demystifying Affects is award winning in marketing and small business service to community.

Chapter 4

Federal Government Freedom of Information Requests and Reviews

Number: *Federal Small Business Admintration-2017-Freedom of Information Act*
Requester Name: *Gregg K. Jann*
Date Submitted: *01/27/2017*
Request Status: *Submitted*

Description: Gregg K. Jann of Santa Rosa, CA and educated one time at Chico State University and Sonoma State University, with much at Santa Rosa Junior College education, feels in a non-fiction book published that he who is author of this request copy righted "https://www." used in starting internet addresses and that he applied this code from his early family dynamics to point to secret code like a mothers diary or warnings to not talk like in wartime or econ deals. Does Small Business Administration have record with Commerce

Department or any government entity that Gregg Jann contributed computer code used for internet, his peace themes are worthy of respect, and Gregg was stolen making his education presentations correct in asserting he was stolen as a vulnerable entrepreneur and student rights enterpriser. Gregg Jann wrote a diagram at the CSU, Chico library in mid 1980s before the internet was invented stating how he could design a computer to be more readable on screen, while his story says he was handed a drafting paper and he drew it out here at Chico, and then at SSU in front of another student he typed in the surrounding of "htttp" inclusive of aforementioned code and it's not hypertext markup language without Gregg Jann. Gregg Jann planned to market his international peace attempts, perhaps US President Reagan speechwriting, his AIDS naming, and even his luck in riding the Subway in attention getting manner all in the mid-1980s except SSU from '92 to '94.

Tracking Number: *Federal Department of Commerce-2017*
Requester Name: *Gregg K. Jann*
Date Submitted: *01/25/2017*
Request Status: *Submitted*

Description: Was or is Gregg K. Jann taken as a source of capitalism endeavors including business, movies, and political interests as method to steal Intellectual Property meant for value to Mr. Jann but given away perhaps for political fundraising or US Presidential legacy of individual/group administrations since US Presidents during 1980s, even with help of Stanford or Hoover Institute or US Western computer firms? Gregg Jann graduated from Chico State University 1986, Sonoma State 1994, and Santa Rosa Junior College in 1982. He was a business, economics, and computer science student in commercial applications creating famous wordsmiths since young and was a published newsletter/newspaper writer spreading righteous indignation and Protestant reform even peace and justice in his view. Gregg Jann was an elected official in education starting with Clinton's term in '98 after serving on the Democratic Central Committee of Sonoma from 1994 to 1998. Mr. Jann was Chair of the Sonoma County Mental Health Board also from 1994 to 1998, and established his mental health care reputation beyond consumerism while working 10 years at CSN from 1999 to 2009, while working in government tax raising pre-company designing a tax act of Prop 63(the Mental Health Services Act of California) which passed and is the impetus to propel The Honorable Gregg Jann to be registered in Marquis Who's Who of America, Health Services Section. Gregg Jann was to lead Social Security policy to enable business owners to work lightly into retirement, making a kinder and gentler nation with power. Mr. Jann's ideals were recognized in a short editorial in Hispanic Business magazine from Santa Barbara shortly after his election after appointed office. This message is to confirm your request submission to the FOIAonline application: View Request. Request information is as follows:

Tracking Number: *Federal Communications Commission- 2017*
Requester Name: *Gregg K. Jann*
Date Submitted: *12/28/2016*
Request Status: *Submitted*

Description: WAS Gregg Jann on New York City TV as a subway survivor during the mid 1980s Summer? Gregg K. Jann visited his father, who worked uptown Manhattan at 475 Riverside Dr. Gregg K. Jann was a Chico State University student who came in a flight from San Francisco, and returned on a special airplane to SFO or nearby. Gregg Jann was uncertain the entire time of this incident, and wants verification and words that Gregg Jann was on television in NYC or on training films by playfully pounding his chest upon emergency arrival at an underground station. The camera picked up no teeth, and Gregg Jann had tetracycline stained teeth at the time, now presentably white. After Gregg K. Jann was playing a "stowaway" in the back seat of his father's commute transportation vehicle from New City, Rockland County, Gregg found the subways under Columbia University were running without fully stopping. Gregg Jann's father Reverend Donn G. Jann did minimal instruction about survival and Gregg was experiencing New York City without his dad's permission or knowledge until Gregg arrived at his father's underground parking structure en-route to this fateful trip. Gregg Jann seems now after accurate and important re-memory process of his own with help and a television replay to remember jumping onto the slow moving subway and walked in it, changing subway cars. Gregg saw a crowd of people at one of the exits of the subway, and a white ribbon wrapped around the emergency exiting passengers. A person said "like a knight" as Gregg Jann grabbed the upper back of a swooshing passenger in the crowd jettisoning out of the runaway onto an exit landing. The TV showed Gregg Jann strutting and stated a reenactment and replayed on his TV screen at his home circa 2012 or so in Santa Rosa, CA (still current address) is portrayed in one sentence in his book A Jann Plan:Creative Origins Advocacy/ Teach Peace and Creative Accountability, published at Rose Dog Books (Dorrance Publishing, Pittsburg, Pa) and on the back cover.

From: Gregg Jann
Sent: Wednesday, September 21, 2016 1:51 PM
To: Sales Rep Author Services
Subject: plagiarism of A Jann Plan by online dictionaries harming efforts to recover ownership

I wrote "original naming lark" of this disease on the back cover of A Jann Plan published 12-1-14 World Aids Day. In the last chapter or the next to last chapter, I include my mental health services blog entry on a Foreigner concert in writing early 2014 with First and Original Song Larking of a specific song of "I want to know what love is."

"Larking" was not in online or paper hard copies of published dictionaries when I wrote and advocated this concept for myself to be recognized legally worth money value and control to be used to recover credit and ownership of my source perspective designer creations. Now "lark" is quoted in Google and some other online dictionaries last I complained about this copyright infringement to mean "enjoy oneself" instead of hard, creative bouncing and initializing capitalist endeavors where people found I was a good source for "AIDS" to songs and movies to the internet: see my book non-fiction A Jann Plan.

I copy right on my own soon few months after I wrote my blog entry then sent off my manuscript for my 2nd published book thankfully to you at Dorrance Publishing and Rose Dog Books in Pittsburg, PA and you followed up with a complete copyright.

2) Also, I FO(first and originally) spoke "poontang" for women as object as a youth in the 60s on my own make up for my attitude including too decent to say "pussey" which all the men and youth football players on my teams said. I saw a movie Bonfire of the Vanities weekend ago on HBO on demand and see Tom Woolfe is stealing my work, verbal copyright, and invading my privacy with slander and false definition etymology of the history of this particular word changing words previously used in the South.

Can you help me to protect my copy right for my word naming credit as important as AIDS and SEX, for my money to me particular when my book A Jann Plan boils down to piracy of innocent good character up to and including Luther Burbank of Arbor Day reaching across continents in words not just internet source perspective designer and his computer code of https//www.

Sent: Tuesday, February 16, 2016 3:43 PM
To: Author Services Rep
Subject: "For sources" any awards for A Jann Plan author?

Is Dorrance Author (Rose Dog Books) Gregg K. Jann worth a "for Sources" lifetime achievement Pulitzer? Current blog entry at Jannda.com is tilted "Doctor's Punishments for Not Liking" is part of A Jann Plan and credit of journalism like the school that is Columbia University. Gregg is looking for starts and larks of parts of movies and more in pursuing action that may be closed files now due to corruption of government, non-profit organizations and television industries. My file for A Jann Plan was closed to Pulitzer too same year I published the book, and can we reopen files for rights of winning?

Political commentary in mental health with health business license uncovering in blog online writing continuing and 2 books sources of capitalism and words. Through medicine punishments are worth awards when determined Gregg Jann writes non-fiction and is a counselor, sole proprietor trademarked.

Gregg does not write standard format, as he did not study English composition in college degrees according to passing CLEP for CA State Universities. Jann is a survivor of horrific processing and triumphant life sacrifices not wished, and wrote a philosophy book to his name.

Gregg withheld saying he named AIDS first and originally coming out now as straight heterosexual, and even government may not have known it was Gregg Jann the way he did it. We see enough non-fiction to his first and originals at Rose Dog Books for A Jann Plan, and his new, nude credits suggested on Prabook.com are striving to reach maturity as good as bonds for Mr. Jann's income.

Can you comment to me if you think I am worth for sources recognition in journalism awards and book writing for A Jann Plan and Jannda.com.

To: Book Store Owners of the San Francisco Bay Area
01/09/15 at 2:12
A Jann Plan by Gregg K. Jann, ISBN: 978-4809-1722-4
Publisher Rose Dog Books from Pittsburg, PA. Non-fiction categorized in law-economic-mental health sold online at publisher under Education and Parenting for author's leading kindness in policy with counseling.
Full title: A Jann Plan: Creative Origins Advocacy/Teach Peace and Creative Accountability
Listed at Books in Print, Baker & Taylor and Ingram Lightning Source.

Marketing: Perhaps a book signing suggested by one store manager in January/February/March or soon after for book published December 2014!! Santa Rosa author, resident since 1967, with address and work experience in San Francisco, East Bay, and Marin and Sonoma County, and in Sacramento ballot advocacy.

Please order A Jann Plan, Creative Origins Advocacy/Teach Peace and Creative Accountability by Gregg K. Jann for your store. The book focuses essays on mental health written by a Marquis Who's Who in America blogger, counselor, and former elected official in education. A Jann Plan reveals starting origins of many famous endeavors worth etymology; in music, Hollywood, Silicon Valley, and in legislation. Author claims he is first in naming for the disease AIDS in a serene letter to the Medical Association coming out of hiding. Advocating for a more authentic economy with more justice to source perspective designers and origins, the book contains Jann's 2nd ballot proposition suggestion TP/CA. A Jann Plan includes other legends besides thc ledger-domain starts, like bear wrestling in Banff to his never revealed before testimony allegedly surviving the Trail Side strangler of Mt. Tamalpais. Only in A Jann Plan is about this back packing incident in Point Reyes while a high school sophomore at Montgomery high school. We can prove matters with significance and book sales, and we need to know his Reagan speech making FO (in Chico's Whitney Hall dorm bathroom) for foreign policy and well as inventions herein.

To Collections Manager, Sonoma County Library
Subject: Form submission from: Suggest a Purchase
Submitted on Thursday, January 8, 2015 - 11:29am Submitted by anonymous user: [50.193.39.30] Submitted values are:
ISBN: 978-4809-1722-4
Title: A Jann Plan, Creative Origins Advocacy/Teach Peace and Creative Accountability
Author/Performer/Composer: Gregg K. Jann
Publisher: Rose Dog Books, an imprint of Dorrance Publishing Publication Year: December 1, 2014
Format: eBook
Audience:
Adults, Teens
Comments: A Jann Plan by Gregg K. Jann focuses on mental health. The non-fiction book writes he is the source designer of famous works and words, with a ballot initiative suggestion distinctly different and combining Gregg Jann's design of the Mental Health Services Act. Jann came out of hiding and quietness for his First and Original AIDS namesake in 1982 and the Trail Side Strangler incident he lived at Point Reyes while a Montgomery sophomore, both experiences in his book as well as a brief sentence mention on a runaway New York subway in the 80s. Author is former local elected school official at Piner-Olivet USD, and resident of Santa Rosa since 1967. Gregg Jann is a Marquis Who's Who in America, Health Services Section honoree as a counselor/businessman. He writes a blog in advocacy of mental health at Jannda.com, where his mental health career started as Chair of the Sonoma County Mental

Health Board and he opened up Interlink. Mr. Jann has represented the county in appointments and election services, most currently the Waterways Advisory Committee of the City of Santa Rosa. Jann has worked throughout the county in recent past for his Route Salesman in frozen food and green contracting canvassing. Jann's first book is in philosophy and political science titled Bettering the World. Jann has gone to local schools in kindergarten from Village, Slater, Montgomery, the Junior College, and Sonoma State and graduated with his first BS from Chico State.

Google: User Reviews:

A Jann Plan was reported to author as "the best book on the subject." Using a mental health focus to educate and de-stigma reader, Chapter 2 is about lost intellectual property and with a correction with claimed origins in the first person of a vulnerable entrepreneur and official. Yet our economy does not reward first and originals, or consumers of mental health for that matter, so Chapter 4 is a ballot initiative suggestion starting with the fertile creative state of author's home state of California. A Teach Peace goal for schools in character education was excerpted from author's school board work at Piner-Olivet USD in Santa Rosa, CA. Author added Intellectual Property reforms to include more titles in entertainment and productive enterprises, and more people to have monetary rights to include youth, disabled, and more creative type people in general. This is author's 2nd published book on political commentary with many hidden legends experienced in real time over the author's life span in Northern California. And surviving train wrecks in New York and Washington state, both suspicious knight hood type jousting over the author's genesis roles in internet and consumer economy like LinkedIn and design before a doctor did some forgetting measure while author was a student during Reagan era making "larks" of origins of Mr. President speeches as the book can assert in non-fiction formats.

Amazon.com: Customer Reviews
Top Customer Reviews

5.0 out of 5 stars

Mental Health Counselor Survives with Legendary Background for Sources in Economy By Gregg K. Jann on September 28, 2015 Meant for the book to be picked up and read anywhere starting on most any page, A Jann Plan glimpses into the mental health world from a champion's viewpoint. A different look than straight ahead psychology, the author shares an end viewpoint and as a counselor surviving a horrific process to bring to us origins of famous works and words. Source perspective designs need recognition, support, and reward - now with author's second published book Western Economy is called into action as the East may have done using espionage unknown to author. Instead of pirating the vulnerable as Reagan's men may have done to a speech maker before author could strengthen his toe hold on designing the internet, the author advocates US and California for Teach Peace and Creative Accountability for character education in schools, IP reform for the lawyer, customer service to understand the tenuous strength of origins, and to honor verbal copy rights like in office or in promotions at work. Author Gregg Jann has been an elected and appointed local government official serving nearly 2 decades, and denies he was a Reagan Black Out case although Mr. Jann did tell college dorm mates he was too legendary for just Reagan speaker (read the book).

Amazon.India: Top Customer Reviews

5.0 out of 5 stars

Safe Harbor Economy an Answer to IP Theft Grandly By Gregg K. Jann on 27 September 2015 Reporting to author stated by a fellow Christian Methodist church member seated next to him that A Jann Plan was "the best book on the subject." Author focused on mental health, with his introduction in A Jann Plan about trusts and holding for someone vulnerable particularly. A Jann Plan has measures and ballot initiative suggestions for a "safe harbor" economy, without spelling out "safe harbor" or "un-Pirating capitalism" so as not to inflame the legal authorities. Origins of famous works and words are in book, and we can see with A Jann Plan there is an answer to defend against too much theft of creative enterprises with many solutions presented in book from the source perspective designer role of author.

New Keynesian Economics some Laissez-faire

Submitted on Mon, 2016-11-07 14:44

Intermediate Macroeconomics class while enrolled in my Graduate School degree/2nd BA program in Business Economics led understanding the economy for jobs was best for mental health. We need to protect a Safety Net economy as fueled by the engines of Capitalism.

The ISLM curve designed after Keynes provides proof that government spending expands the economy more than tax cuts have a plus effect. Any Econ major who tells you different is all for himself or just greedy in his view. Don't exclude yourself by advocating for the best aggregate economy. Jann Demystifying Affects does not abuse 'for me."

Property Rights and Ethics

We Add to Smith's "Invisible Hand"

Submitted on Sat, 2016-12-03 18:23

Adam Smith wrote modern foundations of capitalism 3 times to follow the "invisible hand." This is business doing what business does. Not shoulds or needs particularly and not to "you" coinciding basis in Christianity. Self -interest for each part making a greater whole, maybe meaning just one is the entire picture of a unit's responsibility in our business times.

Greater care in health to family and beyond, more understanding with empathy, and better human rights mostly abroad are best advocacy with opportunity. Government, non-profits, and kinder employees can continue differences even Trump Time.

Property Rights and Ethics

Trust in Person not Forced Treatment

Submitted by Gregg Jann on Sat, 2016-01-16 15:00

Forced Treatment may for a time put medications into a mentally ill person who meets the definition grave disability, or hurting himself or others for Involuntary Commitment laws. I opposed FT when appointed to Cal Net to take part of that organization's ideology.

In my own opinion, long held and consistent with my work and life experiences, is that Forced Treatment causes fear and a lack of progress on freely understanding the needs of consumer's person. Consumers need good habits and kind support with coaching to include them to get through unknowns or difficult passageways from obscure to task management like work.

Consumers free will, with staff persuasion selling to accept supports builds trust because you included the healthy person part prevalence - like checking in with anybody will include their offered participation to gain likeability and honest trust. Author is a coach, former social rehab counselor by paid position.

Advocacy

Freedom and Cleaning Apartment

Submitted by Gregg Jann on Tue, 2015-12-29 14:25

Keeping your house clean is great, for you and your guests. It's vital to have thoroughly clean bathrooms, kitchen, and floors if you have family staying over. It is a sign of independence that you can keep your hygiene up and aren't too lazy to keep germs away. The deep cleaning of refrigerator smudge, or dusting window sills and baseboards caked on with dirt behind heavy furniture can require assistance.

In Home Support Services is for Medi-Cal eligible residents and requires an assignment of a social worker complete with annual house inspections. A simple maid service free of social services for janitorial work for deep cleaning less regular than every other week can be hired when someone doesn't have the gumption to thoroughly keep on top of cleaning.

Sounds like a New Year's Resolution is in order to keep your place thoroughly cleaned, for independence and if money is wanted for TV and internet, any other necessary expenses.

Motivation

Memo: "Gumption" is the word from my childhood that the Hollywood feature movie Forrest Gump is based on. I seem to remember walking into a Sonoma County non-profit where its ED was also about filming and theater, along with restorative justice at least for the young who are teenagers. I was on the spot appointed to the Advisory Board for to have eyes and ears. When looking back I described a movie using my "gumption" words on myself always running for election, and specifically mentioned making a move with a wide span of history a little older than myself in depicting the Vietnam War scene that Oscar likes, combined and the love of chocolate spurred on by the love of my mother. I think I "larked" the movie title and synopsis with plot to a gaffer who was Administrative Secretary of this non-profit or was it the ED? I stated the title but I am hazy about clarity and not my standing as a writer. I want a good gaffer who wants to prove at least one starring actor keeps taking from me without telling me or she likes me even stealing from my recently passed mother. I am trying with my trueness building my new, nude credits to be used commercially with liking attached to Gregg Jann. I think also as I have previously stated that I was stolen for Bear Revenant Methodist for my bible study and mother, both with me and not telling me we are designing another pin to my churches sign meaning more than just me, this time for revering the environment as strong as nuclear disarmament in this world.+ Other movies in A Jann Plan are worth performance and payment to Gregg Jann in Oscar winning for new property rights.

Dear Military Personnel and Counsel:

I would like to appeal my FOIA Request sent February 19, 2016, after then originally sent to Headquarters Marine Corps FOIA and received on February 29, 2016 **re Oprah Winfrey show and my official military recruiters visit at college grad time.** My request is being controlled under file number DON-USMC-2016-. Can my request be considered a "perfected" FOIA request if necessary to get it completed and finished, and can your agency create records and determine my request is vital in USA interests? It concerns truing False Origin re: my Intellectual Property lawyer, to respond to Gregg Jann. Please inform me if remembered and followed up on by Military or staff.

Local recruitment records may not have been set up in the first place for my brief office visit to the all recruiting station at the Federal Building on Sonoma Ave in Santa Rosa, CA in Winter or Spring 1986, or even if my name was documented. Can Counsel research and investigate, from Archives to staff memory to inform me if my visit that one fine day was extraordinary and memorable to Navy personnel or any other military present as all branches were working with say **"Oprah Winfrey."** I am alleging I was forwarded to bigger fishes eating smaller one making hand over fist in money **from Oprah Winfrey forming to** (partial list) my internet inventiveness angle in code and peace theme, to Soviet Union retiring and getting smaller from Reagan speaker first and originally, to enterprises coming from New York news attention of my subway ride I didn't know at the time but shown on my TV as stated in A Jann Plan. I am remarkable in stating or writing beginnings and synopsis of missions, movies, songs, and legislation all not proven making usury of me and avoidance of management feedback to me as entrepreneur and Reagan speechmaker starting with AIDS name and acronym from Gregg Jann (same) first and originally.

I make many of my genesis claims in a 2nd non-fiction social science, law, education, and economic book published in Pittsburg, PA at Dorrance Publishing, my work's particular imprint for A Jann Plan at Rose Dog Books under Education and Parenting on RoseDogBooks.com. **SEE PAGE 10 for TOPIC OF FOIA OPRAH WINFREY SHOW ON TV within A Jann Plan: Creative Origins Advocacy/ Teach Peace and Creative Accountability by Gregg K Jann.**

I fulfill some needs in my work and life claiming to be worth one or more medals from Federal Government, so don't be impeded by the subtitles of my book in your willingness. People don't advocate, or care about origin credit, and deny mental health consumers or paraprofessionals too easily, and public employees can't manage well compared to business education that I have obtained so I am unique and special for policy and work kindness leadership. I have proposed existing solution first and originally to end gridlock in the CA state legislature over funding streams that exist currently because of my advocacy work first and originally when I was moonlighting jobs and wanting to be money via politico and counseling labor as fields in my great IP words and works. I need rightful credit, and not taken advantage of, and to pay me extremely well for extremely important widely used IP that funded counties throughout the state of CA: **this FOIA Request alleged starting of a television and media empire out of Chicago that I met a BD/stand-in of PRA later**.

My appeal should be granted for it is in this request, I say I started **"Oprah Winfrey"** television and media empire based in Chicago, IL by describing theme mission along with the word choices for title pay and also told recruiters that I wanted to invent peer counseling because of mental illness, schizophrenia, and sickness I saw in military men on a television program during my high school era 77-80. My appeal should be granted for starting origins are important and new credits with money to Gregg Jann to follow make more honest capitalism for USA which is authentic and special both each priceless and valuable in monetary. I am not saying Oprah does peer counseling like I can do and was doing in past, as her entertainment license has a different focus. My social rehab experience for 10 years including adding consumer labor rights to a union contract, now having a health business license and I have professionally registered a mental health services trademark at the US Patent and Trademark Office for Jann Demystifying Affects is work too in my disabled work life. I write a blog on mental health read a little internationally not just Facebook for my company JannDA, provide speaking engagements and trainings not just A Jann Plan book promotions but for the largest non-profit nationally about mental illness, and try to collect intellectual property making new inroads in tax law at the CA state level and trying to be remunerated to IP use in past and present. **Neither I nor my sole proprietorship has been getting credit from managers who should pay contributors.** Also for the country I am trying for history remarks in Gregg Jann's name worth textbooks to be more than money with out un-money to me as the source perspective designer of greatest history making in America from myself Mr. Gregg Jann, The Honorable Gregg Jann, perhaps "grassroots Gregg" for extraordinaire.

I am a former elected official for the school board 98 to 6/05 and former Chair of the Mental Health Board 94 to 98, and appointed and elected in politics and civics. I am in Marquis Who's Who in America under Health

Services for being registered as a significant accomplisher with ethics.

Staff Sergeant, across Courthouse Square from my home and lap top computer most days, was asked to read my *Another Claim* entry on page 10 of A Jann Plan, where she and **TOPIC** is named particular in my search for honest credits and an authentic capital large-size for Gregg Jann. She read silently in front of me and that was my second time to see the US Army recruiting office in Santa Rosa, CA in the past few years. She called me an "Army Officer Candidate." My previous US Congress Rep staff heard I asked if I was spied on and that I was the President's "August Tip" in capturing Osama bin Laden in President's speech. I asked my new Congressman Field Director if I could win a medal, a new credit, and money like I did ask the President too, and both CA Senators.

Sincerely,
Gregg K. Jann

Freedom of Information Act Requests: No Record or No response to Jannda.com

Chapter 5

Final Words Not Yet Painting

Mourning with Smart Closure

Submitted 2-6-17 at 14:59 CST

Mourning for a relative or close friend who has died is natural. Grief is unhealthy if it goes on too long, even if for a parent if lasting years. Verbally sharing with the deceased while the dearly departed lived will reduce grieving if done well for closure.

Near their death, tell to their understanding how important this person was to your life. Her mentoring, that you now feel a life enveloped by her surroundings, or reminding her of having the fun activities together especially if due to her effort from childhood to family building are important to express in person.

Family and Friends Property Rights and Ethics Closure has to be done smartly, as something we don't apply the word "smart" to usually. Positive, forward-looking summary like goodbyes if she only hears from you instead of further visiting that does not sound like the end or final ominous, heavy hearted energy you give her.

I loved Mom. She died in presence when I was writing in process. She was cut short sooner than we expected in a song/hymn dispute over The Gloria Patri. I wondered to her if I sang this first from my heart to be used Presbyterian over their offering plate placed by my dad Donn. I asked in her well place if I sang it first and originally then executed by my dad without knowledge except I may was on track to Prophet. "It was a little earlier" she said. I read at his church the copy right is 1662 like a good date for me in playing games. I would ask Great Britain if I could if book date is a lie. Mom accepted something and we, her family, wanted her to live longer. I daily was setting by her side gingerly last months of her life after years of taking her to church and hosting Sunday meal.

I honor both my parents for all with they provided and the care I took, including that of my other family members. To the world of background both I was raised and remain, just Thank you, unless my National Merit scholarship was stolen too along with the larks I created for entertainment, company, and Political and Care Leg not yet on contract basis taken from my awareness.

I had a vision in a mustard field about Jesus suffering and not wishing his name be used for evil during the 60s. Jesus was taller, around 6 feet 1 inch, and wailed this to me audibly when I was alone. The evil he spoke conveyed meaning heard to my ears that he said as quote "war" to me. Maybe his plan for me was for the environment and ecology in Christianity conservation and appreciation for beauty as Jesus gently touched a yellow mustard flower remaining on its stem between Jesus's fingers. This was during my primary elementary education early years, and I was across the street from my home. Jesus was black and grey, dark yet appeared like he was some light in his look to him. Later when I was a teenager in the bushes on the Pt Reyes bluff I never compared this His sighting to the campsite intruder who was embodied of my warning of fear and danger. Did dad think I was worth prophet and to take a turn as poor Gregg, which I opine for authentic ownership for economy and if we can solve mass destruction weapons and so on with our rival and enemies. I stepped through one well, did he write me in the bible which I did not do. I believed even C.O.'s had a right to defend themselves, and wasn't sure if those in charge would feel the same way. I did criminal justice in civil defense against gay rape and mass murderers' pattern, even a cult religious conspiracy, and may have gotten punished or naturally so. Author had many whiteouts, suppressions, and repressed memories of bravery, adventure, and unknown beautiful sexes with writing to recovery and reclaim to himself and value and leadership.

I'm sorry if court ever determines I lie about awards when I hardly ask for them. They are good ideas if not too much usury as in not informing the recipient. I don't see as much design and bona fide wordsmithing from a Mental Health Advocate as I have done for decades in California and beyond. I am surprised by my rediscovery how much journalism, colleges, governments, and health care do not know about the psychiatric disabled and also my contributions due me unless they are hiding (again from Book II starting with Book I now here in Book III) "The Man, The Myth, and The Legend" that Gregg Jann is.

By the way: I told Congress at a SSU public forum in 2016 I was "Beowulf", so there. Anybody think Some Guy who is this work author should be a college provost for Teach Peace curriculum creation and origin reward with development including first and originals' IP and self/family protection from harm? I said these things in Van Gogh for Myself hoping for dough meaning money from all my IP and books. I state I am author of first and originally from me, maybe in the entire world. No one writes or speaks in a vacuum, and isolation of a politico must have a good reason besides religious persecution or stealing Catholic the Old Way for things big and small.

In San Francisco's Right-to-Speak attitude I may have been pulverized by medicine and poison for the right to own credit as a political philosopher spoken when a child. Now I'm an adult. Is it I, Lord, who influences America in capitalism ways and in asking Russia to retire the Soviet Union and for it to get smaller with its people getting bigger in spirituality. Do you want for me to "catapult" safely through the Berlin Wall to continue to be authentic source of a peaceful cease and desist of nuclear stand-off between E and W with the cold war spokesman who is Reagan threatening with an MX missile and taking speakers.

We need especially recovery with enough money to love, when? Its now, feel welcome if you're beautiful female heterosexual and not needing from him a great listener necessary. I want my wishes no longer denied.

Author is an American who works the mental health field as blogger at Jannda.com, former elected official, and current sole proprietor and part time teacher for a non-profit. His care to him, community he makes home, and women he's shy to meet should know Gregg Jann is a beautiful person. His hero story and lifetime legend were unknown until book publication presumably for 1) Democrat speechmaker 1st stolen by other political party 2) USA hurts anyone too moral 3) Straight men are disliked for hire in Sonoma even with Gregg's 2 management degrees and grad training.

CPSIA information can be obtained
at www.ICGtesting.com
Printed in the USA
LVHW040618201222
735554LV00012B/580

9 781958 876428